THE HOUSE

Written by Jane R. Latourette
Illustrated by Sally Mathews

By a river, long ago,
in far-off Galilee,
two men set out to build new homes:
John and Zebedee

They chance to meet along the road,
their donkeys small beneath their load.
"Greetings, Friend! Where are you bound?"
says John to Zebedee, who frowned—

ARCH Books
© 1966 CONCORDIA PUBLISHING HOUSE, ST. LOUIS, MISSOU
MANUFACTURED IN THE UNITED STATES OF AMERICA
ALL RIGHTS RESERVED   ISBN 0-570-06019-2

"Oh, guess I'll look along this side,
right where the river spreads out wide.
I'll find some sand to build upon—
a day or two, I'll have it done!

"And are you going over yon?" asks Zebedee of his friend John.

"Yes, there's a hill-top spot I've found, with bright red flowers all around. From way up high, there's quite a view, and *solid rock* to fasten to."

Each takes his donkey and supplies
and starts to work 'neath fair blue skies,
with river gurgling in between—
the gentlest stream you've ever seen!

Look! Zeb is done in two days flat.
No foundation—he just skipped that.
He doesn't think what might go wrong;
now hear him sing his care-free song:

"Oh, tweedle-dum and tweedle-dee,
no work, just *fun*, for Zebedee.
Get by as easy as I can,
that's why I choose to build on sand!
Oh, I'm the man who builds on sand,
builds on sand,
builds on sand,
Oh, I'm the man who builds on sand,
come dance and sing with me!"

For many days, beneath the sun,
John's family works to get theirs done.

Foundation first—and then the blocks,
with songs that ring across the rocks.

To celebrate, when work is done,
they join their neighbors for some fun.

A feast, some songs, some games for all;
but say—those clouds look like a squall!

Lightning zig-zags 'cross the sky;
the angry clouds come roaring by.
Thunder crashes—the rain begins—
great gusts of rain, pushed by the winds.

John's family runs for home, pell-mell;

Zeb's family, frightened, starts to yell.
"What shall we do? What shall we do?
Look, Pa, the river's rising, too!"

They scramble to the second floor,
but still the water rises more,
and slowly swings the house about,
this way—that way—There's no doubt

they need to clutch at some loose log,
and hold on tight, all four—and dog!

John's house shakes some, and slightly sways,

but on that rock it stoutly stays.

He suddenly sees his neighbors' plight, he rushes down from his safe height, and pulls Zeb's family on their log straight in to shore—all four, with dog!

Now, warm and snug, they all look out
upon the flood, and round about.
Of Zeb's new house there's not a trace;
just water now where was his place.

He shakes his head, does Zebedee,
"Why did I act so foolishly
to think a house could stand
if built on nothing more than sand?"

A brilliant sun comes bursting through,
and makes a rainbow—what a view!
The bright red flowers merrily
lift up their lovely heads to see.

And the river settles back to its old familiar track.

Dear Parents:

Our story is based on a parable Jesus told about His teachings. When a person hears what Jesus has to say and bases his life on it, he will be like a man whose house has a solid foundation. No floods can undermine it; no winds can sweep it off.

But the man who hears what Jesus says, yet lives as if it had nothing to do with him, builds on a shallow and flimsy foundation. His life is headed for a disastrous surprise.

Can you help your child understand the point of the story? And will you help him build his life on solid rock, not by threats, but by the way you guide him and shape the life of your family?

THE EDITOR